Michael

HAPPINESS

IN FIVE MINUTES A DAY

Be Happy

Reading Your Dreams

VINCE CHILES

*5

Printed in the United States of America

ISBN 978-0-9796454-0-2

Second printing

Contents

FOREWORD

IF YOU ARE LIKE me and believe happiness is essential to finding meaning and purpose in your life, this book will help you create and sustain an increased level of happiness. For me a purposeful life has always seemed to be the driving force behind our existence.

My life has not always been one of great purpose. However as I look back on my life it is the combination of all my experiences which allowed me to write this book. Early in life I conquered my greatest challenge. Throughout adolescence and early adulthood I struggled with the seedy world of drug abuse and alcoholism. Addiction robbed me of everything I valued - my integrity and values, my ability to make a living. When I drank I did incredibly stupid things like drive drunk, and became violent and suicidal.

Thankfully I finally hit my bottom and survived a stronger person. On April 24th, 1986, after drinking and smoking marijuana for nearly eight hours, I was arrested for drunk driving and possession of marijuana. With this arrest my worst fear came true. Up to this date I had convinced myself I could have both professional career and live a life consumed by drugs and alcohol. My arrest was one of my first pivotal "light bulb moments" when I first realized having a criminal record and pursuing a professional career would be impossible. Despite the ruin addiction had created in my life, I still held onto to the hope that one day I would be able to complete college and become a professional. I would have a life with purpose and meaning. This arrest appeared to be the damnation of my goal, but in reality it was the event which changed my life. Fortunately the court ordered drug and alcohol treatment vs. jail. In treatment I had to face the cold honest facts about my ruined young life. I recognized that I lied to everyone dear to me and, most importantly, myself. I realized that if I ever wanted to have any dignity and purpose in life, I would first need to free myself from the chains of addiction. I am one of the lucky ones. Recovery through the 12 step programs worked. At this writing I have over twenty years clean and sober.

ONE DAY AT A TIME

The twelve step recovery programs taught me that if I were willing to follow some simple instructions "one day at time" I wouldn't have to ever drink or do drugs again. More importantly it taught me a path to success for almost anything. Triumphing over seemingly impossible tasks is best accomplished in a series of small manageable steps. In the first year of my recovery I learned the vital importance of living life day by day. Additionally, I learned that simple techniques like asking my higher power for guidance and strength each morning and thanking him each night allowed me to accomplish a feat that previously seemed impossible – to stay sober.

When I returned to college in the fall of 1987 I began a journey of self discovery. In my prior life I was academically challenged due to a nearly constant drug induced stupor. Now, I had to admit to myself that I wasn't stupid, but that drugs and alcohol had kept me from realizing my academic potential. For the first time in my life I earned a 4.0 average. This accomplishment was no easy task; I had to re-learn nearly everything, and that required an incredible amount of effort. I needed to teach myself how to concentrate, read, and write all over again. One of the very first things I remember learning was if I broke things down into small increments I could absorb more information and not lose my train of thought. This ability to break things down into small manageable portions when I studied mirrored the lessons I had learned in my personal recovery from addiction. I learned simple tools that helped me stay abstinent "one day at a time."

LIGHT BULB MOMENTS

Time and time again in my personal life I had seen the results of what I'd like to call light bulb moments. When I focused my attention on my strengths or the consequences of a set of negative behaviors I instantaneously gained the motivation to change. In my professional life I have helped clients have similar realizations. Within those moments they found the energy to focus their attention and take proactive steps to change their self-destructive patterns. These light bulb moments always seem to occur instantaneously.

A classic light bulb moment in my life occurred eighteen years ago when I wanted to get into shape. My goal was to exercise thirty minutes a day three times a week. I really didn't know how to exercise. I've never been very athletic, so joining a health club was too intimidating. My light bulb moment was to begin exercising for one-minute three times a week. I found an exercise book I could use at home as my guide. With my exercise book in hand I began an exercise routine that consisted of doing one-minute of exercises three times a week. I thought, "Anybody can do a minute of exercise. Even I can do one-minute of exercises." In two to three weeks I had found it was very easy to adjust to five minutes of exercise three times a week. Within one to two months I had accomplished my goal of exercising thirty minutes three times a week. I was getting into shape, and as a bonus, was feeling confident enough to join a health club. My light bulb moment worked! By putting my awareness into practice I learned that I could change the perception I had about myself that I wasn't athletic. By setting a goal and taking small steps towards accomplishing it, I was able to get to my goal of thirty minutes three times a week and feel better and more confident about myself.

I 1996 while living in Tucson, Arizona and working as a hospice social worker my wife and I discovered that we were infertile. Though today there are options for infertile couples who want children the emotional and spiritual blow of knowing I would never father my own child was hard for me to fathom. This new revelation challenged me to rethink a fundamental belief I had held about immortality. I had always believed that a guarantee of immortality was connected to one's genetic heritage. While working in hospice I met Eliot Jay Rosen, a fellow social worker who was writing a book on death and dying. He explained that for him writing was like having a child His metaphorical child struck a deeper chord that ignited in me a desire to write.

Having conquered drugs and alcohol, I now faced a new set of challenges—grappling with a search for meaning and purpose of life in light of my infertility. I saw Eliot's logic for writing as a worthy path for figuring out my own spiritual quest. Writing would help me discover the answer I sought and quite possibly, help others who were searching for similar answers.

My work in hospice taught me of the incredible mystery of life and death. However I hadn't discovered any conclusive evidence of immortality. What I witnessed in hospice was how the body physically changed at the moment of death. When a person dies the body remains but the person who lived is no longer present. "Where do they go?" I wondered. Outside of my religious and spiritual beliefs I had no tangible proof that they went anywhere. Believing I would live on in my descendants was my tangible proof.

As I struggled with coming to terms how my infertility affected my spirituality, I became intensely aware of the incredible strength, courage, and love on the part of hospice patients and their families. I saw time and again how love empowered people to do things they never thought they could do for someone who was dying. It was my work in hospice and my experiences witnessing death that fueled a desire to make sense of my own emotional struggles regarding my infertility.

When I heard Eliot talk about his own writing, a seed was planted for mine. I would use the endeavor of writing to attempt to answer my own questions about immortality, and more deeply, the meaning of life. I would seek to organize this information in a book that would help others develop a clearer understanding of their own purpose in life. In retrospect I did not realize what a grandiose idea this was. I just needed a new direction in life, a new course to plot, that would help me figure out what I was struggling with spiritually.

GETTING STARTED

So I started. But how does one start to write a book on such a broad topic when one has never written a book before? For me, the idea of writing a book was like the idea of climbing Mt. Everest, an unobtainable dream. I had always struggled with writing. Writing a book seemed an insurmountable task. It tempted me like trying to grab a brass ring on a merry-go-round.

The original theme for writing was to answer the question, "What is the driving force behind life and energy?" The answer to this question has been sought throughout the ages, and I was naive when I started my journey of discovery. It may have been because many of my formative years were spent in a drug and alcohol induced stupor that I did not know much about the origins of life or the theories of physics. It may have been that my lessons in recovery had propelled me forward, making me believe I could accomplish impossible tasks. Regardless, this journey led me to areas of study I had never dreamed of comprehending. I studied physics, the science of evolution, extinction, and environmental habitats. I also studied philosophy, world spirituality, and psychology. For nearly six years, I was obsessed with finding the answers to this question. At the end of six years I had learned much about how humans seek to perceive that which we call real, but I was no closer to writing a book that could help people understand what was the driving force behind life and energy.

I did learn incredible things about life and the energy behind life, and the nature of scientific discovery. I was able to re-define my own personal beliefs about life, death, and immortality. Some of my greatest lessons seemed to be incredibly simple. For instance I learned that some of the greatest scientific discoveries occurred because of some intuitive guess. Another discovery was that science could tell us how things like life or energy behaved, but not always why something exists. I learned to admire the incredible power of human resilience, our innate ability to overcome great obstacles and make great strides for advancements for the betterment of all. I found time and time again evidence of similarities in world religions on the philosophy of life, and I made peace with my infertility and the struggles I had with my sense of meaning and purpose.

Although I learned much about the operations of life I did not find a means to communicate any of my lessons into a meaningful format for a book—until Moore's seminar. In 2004 I attended a seminar by Thomas Moore, Ph.D., author, theologian, and psychotherapist, on spirituality in psychology. During his introductory comments Moore spoke of writing, and the challenges he faced as an author. He emphasized the importance of clarity and simplicity, two areas that I had struggled with in my own writing.

I suddenly wondered why I wanted to write in the first place. If I could explain the driving force behind life, then I might be able to explain what the purpose of life was. I thought about my own life and the times when I had clearly known my purpose. At each of these times of clarity, I always felt happy about who I was as a person. The awareness that happiness might be the cornerstone of purposeful living was a bolt of lightening – I now knew what my book would be about - **HAPPINESS!**

Next, I contemplated, is there a set of behaviors that could help people achieve and maintain happiness? I identified five exercises that could be done effortlessly. Each exercise was simple to do and easy to understand. These five exercises focused on specific behaviors, that when done at strategic points throughout the day, would produce happiness. My awareness about the immediacy of light bulb moments and the minimum effort to focus attention led me to the answer I sought for my happiness exercises. I could design a set of exercises that could be done with minimum effort and within a minute, and still accomplish the goal of promoting happiness.

Next I asked myself whether these behaviors could be done within a short time. As I have learned repeatedly, it is vitally important to break tasks down to their smallest elements in order to achieve big goals. As a social worker I know meaningful psychological change requires one to focus his/her attention on a set of behaviors that can easily be addressed to achieve the desired change. Most counseling interventions that promote lasting change require a client to change personal perceptions about a problem or situation. It may take someone years to focus their attention on a set of self-destructive behaviors, but only seconds to have enough insight about these behaviors to formulate a decision to change for the better. The ability to pay attention is innate; most of us have the ability to focus our attention on an area of interest, and the time and energy to focus is so effortless it can occur instantaneously.

I have often had my clients do the following exercise to become aware of the power of positive thoughts:

> I encouraged them to close their eyes and take ten deep breaths and say "I can't" again and again ten times. When they were done I asked them to notice how they felt. Then I asked them to repeat this same exercise but this time silently repeat "I can" ten times to themselves Invariably clients reported feeling unhappy and experienced a decrease in energy with the "I can't"

exercise, and reported feeling happy with increased energy with the "I can" exercise.

In a matter of minutes my clients were able to recognize how their own negative thoughts/perception impacted their mood and energy level. The "I can't, I can" exercise helped motivate my clients to use positive thoughts in order to improve their mood and self-confidence. Exercises like this one work quickly with little or no effort because we are able to focus our attention and feel the immediate results of positive thinking. In this example, meaningful change occurred once there was awareness that something needed to be changed. My clients then developed the motivation and willingness to take proactive steps to improve their condition. These steps in turn enhanced their ability to feel more confident and happy.

Finally I wondered if I could design a set of exercises that could be done with relative ease and would be adaptable enough to fit diverse personality styles. I reflected on how I started to get into shape eighteen years prior. What was so great about my exercise program and the rational I used to get started was that anyone could do one-minute of jumping jacks, sit ups, or running in place. I looked at my five happiness exercises and immediately saw different options for three of them that would give the reader an element of choice in designing a program that fit personal preferences. Yes, I would design a program that had easy to do exercises and could fit a diverse audience. Within moments I had a workable outline for this book.

INTRODUCTION

THIS BOOK ATTEMPTS TO tackle a complicated concept, happiness - simply. It does this by reviewing the root causes of unhappiness, and happiness and then instructing you how to use the five one-minute happiness program. This program works by contradicting those behaviors or thoughts that create unhappiness, and reinforcing those behaviors or thoughts that produce happiness. This instruction guide is designed for easy assimilation so that you can feel happier quickly. The descriptions that follow get right to the meat and potatoes of the pros and cons of happiness. I've written this text in a format that is easy to understand and use.

From Thomas Jefferson to neurobiology, what is revealed in this book is a program for promoting happiness through self-management. I will discuss concepts like hedonism, cognitive distortions, and auto-hypnosis, in order to give a general idea on the causes of unhappiness and happiness. Next I will incorporate these concepts into my explanation of the five happiness exercises are and how they promote personal satisfaction. Finally, I will describe for you how to do the five one-minute a day happiness program.

Over the past two decades I have researched psychology and self-help methods for both personal and professional growth. I have been blessed and have often enhanced the lives of my clients with this incredible wealth of knowledge and help. However, from time to time I found myself frustrated with certain techniques. I felt the most frustration with self-help techniques that require an incredible amount of investment in time and money to accomplish the goal of self-improvement. When I set out to write this book, I wanted my advice to be easy to use, require as little time as possible, and not require a huge financial investment. I feel that I have accomplished this task, by creating the five-minute a day happiness program.

You, me, us, we, I, they, them and other personal pronouns I use refer to that part of our selves known as the self-identity or conscious self. You know who you are, by how you relate to yourself. When you wake up in the morning, you tell yourself "get up". That voice saying, "get up" is your self-identity. In psychology there is a theoretical side of self-identities called the unconscious - that part of our selves we don't know or recognize. Some schools of psychology believe that the unconscious is where we stuff all the bad things that happen to us in life so we don't have to deal with them; so we can go on living our lives. Another school of psychology, and the one I subscribe to, believes that the unconscious is a resource of strength. The unconscious self is our unmet potential waiting to be ignited in order that we can reach our full potential. My belief is that the identity and unconscious self work together in order to promote happy satisfied people.

The following material includes personal stories and real life examples of people I've helped. These accounts reveal how this program works with different perspectives. These stories demonstrate innate creativity and resiliency, and the individual's intrinsic strengths that work to promote his/her happiness. The strong connection between happiness and personal survival will be emphasized. These stories will reveal how this connection occurs. As you familiarize yourself with the concepts and stories you may begin to relate to your own experiences – resources that have helped you to cope with difficulties.

The "how to" section of this book is the most technical; it takes you step by step through each exercise. There are fourteen exercises split among five different categories. I will explain the exercise and provide simple suggestions for how to choose and use it. You may elect to begin an exercise as you read through the chapter. If you opt to do these, please try to keep yourself to one minute per exercise and only five exercises a day. Another recommendation is that you stagger your exercises throughout the day. In the last chapter I will share a regimen, some additional ideas about applying these exercises to your everyday life, and how others designed programs that worked for their styles. Feel free to experiment with these exercises.

Thank you for taking the time to believe in your potential to achieve happiness. When we experience happiness we feel free to think and do what we like. Our dreams become possible. Happiness and personal satisfaction allow us to have clarity about our lives as we recognize our potential and purpose in life. My hope for you is that you will have a full and happy life.

In my professional work in hospice there is nothing more tragic then a person at the end of life trapped by bitterness and despair, and nothing more inspiring then someone secure in the love of others, in a sense of personal completion, and peace of mind. These two extremes are the results of the type of choices people make about how they live their lives. We can choose to seek happiness outside of our selves and fail, or look within our selves and succeed!

Chapter I

ERRORS IN THE PURSUIT
OF HAPPINESS

"LIFE, LIBERTY, AND THE pursuit of happiness," is a fundamental statement describing the American experience. When Thomas Jefferson wrote these words in the Declaration of Independence he and his fellow framers were establishing a revolutionary government that placed the rights of individuals above that of the sovereign. Freedom to pursue happiness is paramount to the American dream. To Jefferson happiness was contingent on a style of living dictated by virtue, discipline, and industry.

Robert Darnton, Professor of European History at Princeton University, wrote a poignant essay in 1993 addressing Jefferson's contribution to the Declaration of Independence - "the pursuit of happiness." Darnton compared Jefferson's own philosophy of pursuing happiness with the present day interpretation of this pursuit. He does not address the limiting scope of who was eligible for Jefferson's brand of happiness—white affluent men. He does however speak to the ideals that were set into motion by Jefferson. These ideals have held true with the progress of time and the broadening definitions of who are entitled to the pursuit of happiness.

Darnton asserts that in our current day and age the pursuit of happiness has taken on a flavor of John Locke, who asserted: "life, liberty, and the pursuit of property," was a fundamental right for all people. To Darnton the motivation to obtain material possessions and pursue pleasure is behind most Americans' pursuit of happiness today. He concludes by analyzing how this hedonistic pursuit contradicts Jefferson's original philosophy on how to achieve happiness. His analysis reveals the present day American experience – persons obsessed with comfort pleasures, but ignorant of how to obtain genuine happiness.

The want for more seems to be the culprit behind much of our misery—more possessions, more excitement, more money. If we don't desire more then it seems we desire better: better jobs, better looks, better bodies, and better homes. Have you ever said to yourself, "I'll be happy when I have a new car, own a home, have that great job," only to find that the happiness you gain from these things is less than expected? This cycle of always wanting more and never feeling satiated is called hedonism. Hedonism is the pursuit of pleasure, not happiness. Pleasure is a fleeting emotion. When someone is happy they are able to experience sustained satisfaction in many different levels of their lives. A person in a hedonistic cycle can never truly get what he wants because each event or accomplishment reinforces the desire or need for more. The person's desire for more keeps him stuck, seeking more and more pleasure, but never gaining the understanding of what will bring satisfaction in life.

People who strive to maintain longer and longer periods of happiness through possessions and/or excitement often develop destructive behavior patterns. We all like to have fun and feel pleasure, but some of us lack the ability to discern what actions create personal satisfaction, and which ones promote a potentially addictive pursuit of happiness.

Jesse, a self-proclaimed "jack of all trades but master of none," boasts he has a coffee mug that reads "over the hill and still wild." He states, "Oh yeah, I've done it all, and have had it all, cars, boats, motorcycles. I've even jumped out of airplanes. These things are exciting and fun, but they don't ever bring lasting happiness." Yet, Jesse admits he is happiest when he is working on his next project, buying a car, or engaged in an exciting affair. Jesse is stuck in a hedonistic cycle.

Toni, a self-employed beautician and personal trainer, recalls, "I wanted this cabin in the woods so much. I thought having that home would make me happy. But when I got it, I wasn't happy! It was a lot more work then I expected. Don't get me wrong, I liked being in the woods, I just couldn't live in that little cabin. I was miserable. That house wasn't what was going to make me happy." Toni *thought* that cabin would make her happy, but it didn't.

How about making happiness dependent on a goal that hasn't yet been achieved? Weight loss or a healthier lifestyle

are classic examples. "I'll be happier when I can fit into a size
10" or "I'll be happier when I have 6 pack abs." Or how about
our finances? "I'll be truly happy when I win the lottery" or
"I'll be happy when I can afford an expensive new home."
Most of us find that these repeated efforts never seem to
produce the happiness we desired. As a result many of us just
give up, feeling that true happiness is beyond our grasp, or
its just some cruel lie we are told as children.

Larry, a retired steel worker, states, "I'm a failure. I was
really good at sports in high school. I wanted to be a pro, but
I just couldn't get through school. I stopped playing ball and
went to work." Larry gave up playing the sports that made
him happy. He lived his life wishing he had taken that other
path and wondering what that might have brought him. Larry
defined the reason he never found true happiness as the
unfilled dream of his youth.

Denise never got a fighting chance at happiness. Both
her parents were alcoholics, verbally and physically abusive
and, from age four to sixteen, she was sexually abused by her
father. When she tried to do something new, she was told
she couldn't because she was stupid. Rarely did she receive
any type of praise or encouragement from her parents. If
something annoyed one of her parents, they would yell at
or hit whichever child was closest. Denise grew up in an
environment that stifled her spirit, and produced a defeatist
attitude about life.

Still others struggle finding contentment because their
definition of happiness is contingent on other people. Marilyn,
a retired bookkeeper, states, "I think what would make me truly

happy is knowing my kids were more successful." Marilyn's search for happiness in her relationship with others is not very different then those who feel fulfilled if their bosses appreciate them or lovers show them affection, etc.. However, the people they relate to will not always show them the kindness, love, or the praise they desire, which will leave them feeling hurt, alone, or incompetent. The problem with looking towards others to define our happiness is that we have no control over how others relate to us.

Some unhappy people are clinically depressed. The Beck theory of depression asserts that depression is the result of a chemical imbalance in the brain. This imbalance, Beck theorized, is caused by flawed thought patterns. Beck demonstrated in the late 1960's that depression was often the result of distorted perceptions about oneself, others, and reality. It was these cognitive distortions that caused the imbalance in brain chemistry. Beck developed a system of treating depression that taught his patients how to develop healthy thought patterns. Beck's theory of depression and his approach to treating depression revolutionized how depression was perceived and treated. His work is to this day one of the most effective modes of treating depression.

Another explanation for why people are unhappy is because they get stuck using the same old problem-solving strategies for new problems. A basis for solution directed therapy is that people get stuck in problematic cycles that don't allow them to see alternative solutions to their difficulties.

For people who were stifled as children, or those seeking happiness through the eyes of others, or those who are clinically depressed, or who keep trying to solve their new problems with old solutions it is easy to develop cynical perceptions that the possibility of attaining happiness is a childish idea. For these folks their biggest obstacle towards achieving happiness is their perception about how the world operates. When adults get stuck in behavior patterns and perceptions that reinforce their own limitations they do not have the ability to reach a peaceful state. The cause of their problem is the world they live in - not their errors in judgment. Being unable to think themselves out of their unhappiness box, they fail to take responsibility for finding the path to finding happiness.

Therapeutic interventions, like those developed by Beck and others, help people get unstuck and find new or creative ways to pursue happiness. What these experts believe is that we can learn how to think and do things differently and thus promote happiness. Once people recognize that they have a problem pursuing happiness, they can find new solutions that will promote their ability to reach their goal.

Chapter II

WHAT IS HAPPINESS?

A WORKABLE DEFINITION OF HAPPINESS

HAPPINESS MEANS THE ABILITY to experience joyful feelings or appreciate how fortunate one is in life. We all experience happy moments. Joyous occasions result from the completion of a goal, such as moving out of home, buying a new car, or obtaining a promotion. They may also result from a vacation to a beautiful place, or a romantic evening with your partner/spouse. An unexpected surprise, such as winning a prize, or receiving a gift out of the blue, may create a blush of good feelings when you're feeling down. Sustained happiness for most of us often seems elusive. Happy moments are something everyone has, but maintaining lasting periods of joy is a process few understand. True happiness occurs when we have mastered the ability to reproduce joy over and over again, not just when something good happens.

The ability to master the traits that promote happiness comes partly from our ability to be resilient. Resiliency is the ability to bounce back during times of turmoil. We all have this ability to persevere during difficult times. Resiliency may be the force behind our actualizing unconsciousness. Our unconsciousness is that unknown part of ourselves that propels us forward in life towards our highest potential. If hedonism or some other cyclical problem doesn't trap us, our resilient nature will assure our success.

The solution directed therapy model relies on this belief in our resilient nature. Solution directed therapists believe that people in general are essentially resilient and that if given subtle suggestions they will come up with solutions on their own. These therapists also believe that the solution already exists in our everyday experience, but most of us get stuck using the same old solutions for new problems.

Why do most of us get stuck in problem cycles when a viable solution can be found? The solution directed answer relates to an idea called auto-hypnotic states. Their assertion is that the majority of our time is spent in resilient trance-like states. Think of these auto-hypnotic states as what occurs when driving long distances, or reading a good book. Sometimes we can drive for miles and not have a recollection of what happened in the past thirty minutes. Or maybe we are so interested in our book that we have read for hours, but it only feels like a few minutes. The solution directed model asserts that we spend a lot of our time in these auto-hypnotic states.

Generally, we are snapped out of these auto-hypnotic states when we experience some form of distress or discomfort. My best example of how this occurs is what I call the stubbed toe phenomenon. For example, you are going about your life with a laid-back attitude when out of the blue you stub your toe. The pain associated with the stubbed toe brings you back to the here and now. You turn your entire attention on the pain and think, "Ouch, that hurts! How could I have been so stupid not to see that big rock?" In situations like stubbed toes, our strategies for coping with stress or pain become more about avoiding the next stubbed toe, than about focusing on what we are doing when we aren't stubbing our toes or experiencing problems. When we aren't in the problem cycle we are most likely in a resilient auto-hypnotic state.

The solution directed therapist uses the idea of resilient auto-hypnotic states to redirect attention away from the problem so that the client can find a solution that fits his/ her unique situation. These clinicians believe that we spend more time in our resilient trance-like states then in problem states, but that we have trained ourselves to pay attention to what ails us rather than what cures us. By helping their clients make small changes in how they perceive their problems their clients are then able to find the solution that already exists.

Most of us don't ever recognize these resilient auto-hypnotic states as something we can control. Are there people who recognize the presence of these resilient auto-hypnotic states, and use these states of being to be happier and more satisfied? In his book *Finding Flow*, Mihaly Czikszentmihalyi speaks of women and men that he has found who routinely use auto-hypnosis to their benefit. These people have realized that when their thoughts, feelings, and concentration are in harmony with one another, time passes effortlessly and they feel great. For them there was the recognition that when they were involved in recreational activities, sports, or other activities that they enjoyed they felt different then at other times. As a result of this different feeling, they started to design their lives around this harmonizing sensation. Csikszentmihalyi has dedicated his life to studying people who recognize the benefits of using auto-hypnotic states to produce happiness. They have developed systems of living so that they are routinely able to feel satisfied and happy.

To Csikszentmihalyi, people who use auto-hypnotic states to their benefit possess a self-propelling personality. These are individuals who are self-directed and have developed personal philosophies of life that reinforces their ability to routinely experience happiness. They possess a high level of life satisfaction with an awareness that their routine activities provide opportunities for learning and enhanced intimacy with others. The self-propelling personality is not perfect, but is able to see the silver lining in most clouds and bounce back easily when faced with problems or when under stress.

Those with self-propelling personalities seem to have certain things in common. They all seem to value routine interactions with others as opportunities for learning. There is a passion for learning and an appreciation for their own and others' talents. An organized life-style is of value and they strive to live in this manner realizing that their lives are generally happier. They are creative, and often "think outside the box." Interestingly enough, they are not all wealthy or what would be called highly successful, but they are rich in spirit and satisfied with life. Finally, they often strive to contribute to the greater good in their communities and/or society at large.

Such a person is Thomas Jefferson mentioned earlier. Jefferson's personal philosophy included living by a set of virtues, being industrious in one's daily activities, and loving his fellow man. He felt that when one obtained these goals happiness was the end product. Interestingly enough, Jefferson's philosophy closely reflects the key ingredients that today's happiness experts say are essential ingredient for life satisfaction. Author and psychologist, Martin Seligman, discusses these essential happiness ingredients in his book *Authentic Happiness.* Seligman asserts that happy people possess the Jeffersonian criteria for assured happiness. Seligman emphasizes the importance of Jefferson's idea about virtues promoting happiness. He validates Csikszentmihalyi's thoughts about auto-hypnotic states, and self-propelling personalities. On the matter of virtues Seligman states that those who demonstrate the greatest level of happiness seem to possess the ability to live by six universal virtues.

The six universal virtues are derived from commonalties in world religions and philosophy. These virtues include a love of learning, bravery, loving others, fairness, self-control, and faith in the supernatural. My five happiness exercises work to promote auto-hypnotic states and the six universal virtues, while also counteracting cognitive distortions that prevent people from maintaining happiness. People who routinely report a high quotient of life satisfaction live their lives according to these six virtues. They are able to use these traits when they are under pressure and/or experiencing hardships in order find solutions to their problems.

TEACHING HAPPINESS

We can teach people to be happy, just as Beck has taught countless people how to recover from depression. It is possible to learn to incorporate positive traits into our day-to-day lives. The lessons learned from these traits can help change the cognitive distortions that have created unhappiness. As Beck showed in the late 1960's - depression creates an imbalance of brain chemistry. My happiness program implies that people who are the happiest and most creative experience the benefits of balanced brain chemistry. Living a virtuous life can and does positively influence our brain chemistry.

Neuro-biologists have illustrated how living creatures are hard wired to experience pleasure. On a molecular level within each living cell is a chemical called endorphin, and its function is to create the sensation of pleasure. According to these scientists survival is contingent on our ability to experience pleasure. We are all hard wired to feel good, and to continually seek out those activities that help us experience pleasure. Neurobiology has demonstrated that the release of endorphin in our brains creates neuro-pathways that reinforce our biological pursuit of happiness

A neuro-pathway is created when the same types of thoughts or automatic functions are repeated over and over again. On a cellular level brain cells have connection points called dendrites. Two brain cells meet at what are called synapses.

Synapses are microscopic gaps where electric charges and brain chemicals like endorphin are released from one cell, and sent to another receiving cell. One brain cell is the sender of information, in the form of chemicals like endorphin, and energy and the other cell is the receiver. The brain is composed of seemingly endless chains of these brain cell strands. It is these strands and the process of releasing electrical charges and brain chemicals that create neuro-pathways.

When Beck theorized that depression was the cause of chemical imbalances in the brain, his ideas related to the fact that repetitive cognitive distortions created neuro-pathways which caused the imbalance that produces depression. He developed a cognitive approach towards treating cognitive distortions so depressed people could develop new thought patterns that re-balanced their brain chemistry. His therapeutic approach helped his clients develop healthy neuro-pathways that fostered their recovery from depression.

When we live our lives according to the six universal virtues or recognize our unique strengths and resiliency and/or seek to reproduce auto-hypnotic states we are developing those neuro-pathways that promote balanced brain chemistry. Having and developing a manner of living that is disciplined by virtues and emphasizes our strengths rather then our limitations will promote life satisfaction and an optimistic attitude. Studies on neurobiology indicate that our biological tendency is to seek out pleasure. On a molecular level our cells do not have the ability to discern which pleasurable experience will be destructive or healthy. Our brain cells can only tell us when we feel good. Our job is to be able to develop the healthy behavior patterns that will reinforce balanced brain chemistry.

What the solution directed therapists, cognitive behaviorists, and other happiness experts tell us is that we can alter our behavior and thoughts in order to create optimum functioning. Happiness is not simply an American ideal. Biology, personal attributes, and an ability to be aware of our own behavior and thoughts influence it. Achieving lasting happiness requires personal discipline and a willingness to develop those positive skills that promote balanced brain chemistry.

My five one-minute happiness exercises are designed to help you create a personal program that will allow you to experience greater joy and contentment simply and easily. The five exercises that I have developed are entitled: Wake-up Surprised, Take a Break to Re-energize, Create Something New, Learn Something New, and Be Grateful at Bedtime. Each exercise is designed to help promote virtues, balanced brain chemistry, and emphasize your innate resiliency. Collectively they work to create a daily discipline that will enhance your ability to experience positive auto-hypnotic states. Additionally it will explain how these same exercises counteract hedonism, cognitive distortions, and cyclical problem behavior patterns that prevent us from successfully pursuing happiness.

When it comes right down to it, self-management is a key component of happiness. This is what Jefferson meant by industry as being essential in the *pursuit of happiness*. His brand of happiness was the result of good self-management techniques. Thus far, I've reviewed the primary reasons why people are not happy, and what characteristics promote happiness. I have explained the fundamental "why" about happiness: *Why are some people happy while others are unhappy?* In the coming chapters you will discover what each of the five happiness exercises are and *how* to incorporate them into your day to day life. These ingredients are the ability to be resilient, live life according to certain virtues, and experience the benefits of having your concentration, attention, and feelings in harmony. Additionally I will reveal what these exercises do to undermine the tendencies that create unhappiness.

My program seeks to incorporate the six universal virtues, into five easy-to-use one minute exercises. Overall, it will help you to develop the virtue of self-control. An effective self-management style is equivalent to this virtue. When you live life by the virtue of self-control you embrace the importance of moderation in your thoughts, actions, and deeds. When you are able to consistently perform the five one-minute exercises, you will discover you are managing your life with economy and efficiency.

Living a well managed life also means you will be prudent and humble. When you develop the philosophy that your life requires observation of thoughts and actions in order to modify behavior you are being prudent. Good self-management techniques will promote humility. We exhibit humility when we recognize that we are all in the same boat. We recognize each person needs self-management in order to achieve happiness. When someone is unhappy they lack the ability to regulate themselves. Humility allows us to recognize in them our own vulnerabilities and struggles with the process

of self-management. "But for the Grace of God," is a statement
I learned from the 12 step recovery programs. It refers to the
fact that I could easily become a prisoner of addiction at any
time simply by making a few poor choices. It also refers to the
similarities I share with those who are locked in the shackles
of addiction. Good self-management skills allow us to develop
the virtue of self-control.

In Beck's cognitive behavioral approach to treating
depression, he asserted that interventions that are targeted
to help people overcome depression need to be simple and
easily accomplished. Beck explains that people are depressed
because they lack a personal style of managing their lives.
The solution directed therapists help clients to think in a
different direction, so that the client can tap into his/her own
resiliency and find the solutions that best fit their unique style.
My program is designed simply. I've limited each exercise to
a minute because one minute is just enough time to help you
to start thinking in different directions about how you are
currently managing your life. In one minute you can discover
what your strengths are as well as what areas you need to work
on to improve yourself.

Having the ability to live by the six universal virtues directly
impacts the positive experience of living. My five one minute
happiness exercises will help you understand these virtures and
the impact they have on your life. This program is packaged into
exercises you can use at five strategic times throughout your
day. The following sections will describe what each exercise is
and how they work to promote the six universal virtues. You'll
discover how these same exercises undermine those factors

that prevent people from experiencing satisfaction with life. By the end of these following chapters you will understand what each exercise is and how each exercise will promote your ability to encounter joy in life.

Chapter III

WAKE-UP SURPRISED

Look to this day, for tomorrow is but a dream
and yesterday a memory.
–Sanskrit proverb

LOOK TO THIS DAY! The beginning of each new day is a metaphor for the miraculous mystery of life. The day is born at dawn. The rising of the sun breaks the dark night with the vitality of an amber and violet colored sky. Dawn is a transition between darkness and light. As the sun rises it creates a strict contrast of a blossoming day full of brilliance. As light fills the horizon our vision is able to explore the possibility of our new day. Dawn brings with it an opportunity for new life. Each morning is an opportunity to start life anew.

We literally live life a day at a time. Each day is a very manageable increment in time, and developing a system of welcoming the new day can be a vital tool for promoting happiness. So, as your day reveals itself to you, learn to develop an attitude of wonderment and surprise at its beauty!

In our primitive past our ancestors rose to meet the new day with ritual and respect. Our ancestors recognized the mystery the new day brought as an integral part of their lives. Waking up surprised means we allow ourselves to practice this ancient ritual. When we wake up surprised we welcome the unexpected as an opportunity to learn about ourselves, the world we live in, and others. "Looking to this day" means we have confidence to handle whatever comes our way because we have accepted the unpredictable nature of life.

Our environment is constantly changing. Our universe, world, neighborhoods and homes are in a constant state of flux. What do we do about change? We resist it. We deny it exists. We resent its presence. Rarely do we acknowledge it. Acknowledging change is scary. When we acknowledge change we have to admit that we don't know what is going to happen next. It is easier to be miserable and believe we can prevent change. Many of us would rather live in an imaginary world where everything is predictable. But the reality is that nearly everything in our lives is constantly changing. This misunderstanding about the passage of time and our attempts to predict the future can create cognitive distortions and/or defeatism, when life doesn't go our way. If there is one thing predictable about life it is that life is unpredictable.

Happy people see the beginning of the day as an opportunity. Many have morning rituals or routines that help them focus their attention on how they will use their time in their unpredictable world. Happy people exhibit the traits consistent with four of the six universal virtues when they practice morning rituals. The virtues they display are: love of learning, bravery, self-control, and belief in the supernatural.

A morning ritual exhibits the virtue of love of learning by acknowledging the opportunity each day brings to learn more about the life and living. People can derive the greatest benefit from the new day by developing an attitude of curiosity about the unexpected events in life. They invoke their love of learning in their morning routines. They display good decision making in accepting that the dynamic nature of life provides both opportunities and challenges. Happy people face the unpredictability of life with the virtue of bravery. Even in their darkest moments, they persevere with a confidence that they have the integrity to overcome their hardships. The ability to keep going in the face of adversity demonstrates firmness in the face of uncertainty. Having a morning ritual also reinforces the virtue of self-control. It instills a sense of confidence that we can respond to the unpredictable nature of life. Finally, a morning routine helps happy people experience belief in the supernatural or the ability to look past life's ordinariness. It does this by promoting faith in a beautiful world and passion for life. Some happy people use the morning as an opportunity to express their spirituality and gratitude for the new opportunities each day brings.

Typically the first thought that runs through our minds in the morning are all the things we don't want to do that day, or all the things we have to do before getting to those things we really want to do. Our focus is on the stubbed toe, not on how special it is to be alive, and what opportunity the day will bring. When we "Wake Up Surprised" we will start our days with the belief that we possess the will to self-correct past cognitive distortions that have contributed to our own unhappiness.

This attitude helps build some of the positive traits associated with the virtues of love of learning, bravery, self-control, and belief in the supernatural, while also deterring the cognitive distortions we may have developed regarding the passage of time. By Waking up surprised you will be creating for yourself a strategy to anchor your attention on your happiness goal at the start of each new day.

Before I tell how to work this exercise, I want to tell you a little more about Denise. If you remember, Denise's life was wrought with sexual abuse and neglect as a child, and addiction and mental illness as an adult. When I first met Denise she shared with me that she just got some bad news. On top of being manic-depressive she just discovered she had Post-Traumatic Stress Disorder. She was abstinent from drugs and alcohol for years, estranged from her son who had become a perpetrator of sexual abuse, and was caring for her daughter who had a chronic and life threatening illness. Combined with her mental health, and family issues, she revealed that she suffered from chronic fatigue syndrome and had cirrhosis of the liver.

For Denise, getting out of bed each morning has been both an emotional and physical struggle. She has struggled with depression and despair about the wreckage of her past. Many of the perceptions she has developed about how she experiences life and interacts with others are distorted and reinforce her depression. Yet, despite all her trauma she has a resilient spirit. Denise has developed strategies to overcome many obstacles she routinely faces in her life. Despite her physical and mental limitations she has become a massage therapist with an emphasis on helping those who are chronically ill. She has been married for nearly 30 years and is an excellent advocate and caregiver for her sick daughter. Her ability to learn a profession, maintain lasting relationships and navigate the health care system for her daughter all demonstrate Denise's resilient spirit.

Denise committed to do the four-week happiness program stating "It can't hurt." Listen to Denise's own comments about her experiences with the Wake Up Surprised exercise: "It really helped me change my focus each morning. I realized that I had something to live for each day, and that I was going to make the best of it. It has helped me develop a clearer vision of the person I want to become. Each morning I think about what I need to do today to make this vision a reality." For Denise the Wake Up Surprised statement helped her to dramatically turn her life around.

The Wake Up Surprised exercise is easy to do by reading the following statement. Read this statement slowly each morning. It will take you about one minute to complete. It can be read out loud for a more dramatic effect, or quietly to yourself. If you would like to undergo similar results like the one experienced by Denise here is the wake up surprised statement that will help you succeed:

"This is a totally new day in my mind, body, and spirit;

it is a totally new day in my home, neighborhood, town, state, country, continent, and planet. I have never been here before and will never be here again. As a result I am going to develop an attitude of discovery about my life today. I am going to focus my attention on what's positive and beautifully new in my life today."

Each morning upon rising, start your day with this statement. As you become used to focusing your attention in this way, you will recognize the simple newness of the evolution of your life in your surroundings. Your resilient self and brain will do the work in making these new discoveries, all you need do to benefit from this exercise is to read the statement each morning. In the 12 step recovery programs there's a slogan, "Fake it till you make it." If you're a little skeptical about the power of this exercise or of any to come, please, "Fake it till you make it." I so strongly believe in your resiliency that if you do each of the five exercises each day for the next 28 days you will begin to feel happier well before you are finished.

Chapter IV

TAKE A BREAK
AND RE-ENERGIZE

You can start your day over anytime you choose.
–Anonymous

IN THE SECOND CHAPTER I discussed the idea
that we are biologically programmed to experience
pleasure and the reason is because we are dependent on
certain behaviors for survival. That's why eating, sleeping,
physical activity, social interaction, and sex are all fun
activities. Our brains release endorphin when we are eating,
interacting with our friends, or engaged intimately. Our
brains cannot interpret which act of eating, socialization,
or sex is experienced in moderation to assure our optimum
survival. So when we engage in activities like eating a pint of
ice cream vs. meditating for 30 minutes, our brains release
happy chemicals in both scenarios. However eating ice cream

will only give us a short-lived boost of endorphin that isn't easily reproduced. Whereas meditation will give you a boost of endorphin that can easily be recreated anytime you choose to take slow deep breaths, and clear your mind. Our brain tells us when we experience pleasure, but it can't tell which pleasurable experience will create lasting happiness.

It is our job to determine which pleasurable activities will produce the correct chemicals to allow us to experience lasting happiness, and ultimately to survive. The second exercise of the five one-minute exercises is designed to allow you to replicate happy chemistry while minimizing the effects of imbalances of brain chemistry. The "Take a Break to Re-energize" exercise group will help you jump-start the production of endorphin at a strategic point in your day when you need it.

Instead of reaching for that chocolate, or blowing off some steam at an unsuspecting colleague, these exercises will teach you how to engage in physical activities that will help you respond to stress in positive ways. The re-energizing exercises are designed to help you become aware of how you store up stress in your body. Each exercise is designed to help you release stored up stress in slightly different ways. When you learn how to take a break to re-energize you will be learning to develop healthy patterns that interrupt the build up of stress and tension.

Interrupting the build up of stress is not all we learn from these re-energizing exercises. They will also allow you to recognize your natural tendency to rebound from overwhelming situations. These exercises will help you to learn how to change your perceptions about stressful events. By learning to respond differently to stress you will be better able to succeed in your day-to-day endeavors, and feel more confident.

Stress occurs when we feel threatened in some way. It is our emotional and physiological response to threatening events—since when we are happy our bodies respond and produce happy brain chemistry that enhance our ability to feel better. When we experience stress our bodies perceive that we are being threatened and our brains respond chemically to danger. These chemical responses can make us feel nervous, confused, or out of control. In our primitive past our ancestors needed to escape danger quickly. Our biological make-up evolved to produce chemical energy surges so our ancestors would have the energy to fight or escape in order to survive. This "fight or flight response" to stress can create more physiological problems than solutions in our day and age.

The fight or flight response to stress creates problems because the chemicals released cause us to feel anxious. Under this panicky state we try to figure out why we feel threatened. The answers we come up with often reinforce the negative effects of stress, because we either misperceive the stressful situation, or we have already developed a pattern of defeatism in response these types of events. Either scenario has the potential to create imbalances in our brains that reinforce our own dissatisfaction with our life.

Cognitive distortions and/or defeatism associated with the build up of stress are major causes of unhappiness. If you are under a lot of stress and your boss makes a negative comment, a common cognitive distortion may be to perceive "he's out to get me." When we are managing our stress well we probably would perceive a similar negative comment as "what's bothering him today," or "he's in a bad mood." It is how we perceive the events in our day-to-day lives that influence our own unhappiness. When we learn to change how we perceive stressful events we will be happier people. The re-energizing exercises are designed to give you physical tools to help you better handle stress.

Because of the energy surge caused by fight or flight response our bodies need to release this energy and use it productively. Slow Down, Brighten-up, Lighten-up, and Loosen-up are the names of the four Take a Break and Re-energize exercises. These four exercises are targeted to help you recognize the different ways you hold stress and give you alternate strategies for releasing tension. As you become used to using the re-energizing exercises, you will learn to program yourself to react differently to stress and as a result you will feel happier.

These exercises promote the virtue self-control. By using them you will be a better judge of how to respond to daily events. You will develop new perceptions about what you can do to manage stress. You will be able to notice how you have let little things ruin your whole day in the past, for now you have new tools to maintain your cool when the pressure builds. The resources you gain from this practice will allow your behavior to be consistent and as a result you will have more integrity. One of the physical exercises is designed to help you appreciate humor, and feel the immediate physiological rewards that laughter can produce. Using these techniques will allow you to have better self-control. When you incorporate these physical exercises into your daily routine you will be wiser—and happier. Again, here are the four Take a Break to Re-energize exercises; Slow Down, Brighten Up, Lighten Up, and Loosen Up.

SLOW DOWN

The Slow Down exercise is something you probably already do. Automatically from time to time when things get too intense you take slow deep breaths. Slow deep breathing increases the level of oxygen in your blood stream. Increased oxygen interrupts the fight or flight response. When you take slow deep breaths you are able to think more clearly. This exercise can be done in one minute by taking ten slow deep breaths.

When you breathe deeply you use your abdomen. As you inhale your abdomen extends out and as you exhale it contracts inwards. Here is your Slow Down exercise:

Take ten slow deep breaths to the count of three for each inhale and exhale. Your count can be "in, 2, 3" (with each inhale) "out, 2, 3" (with each exhale) for a total of ten inhales and exhales. Using your fingers to keep track of each breath may help. Ten repetitions at this rate will result in approximately one minute of slow, deep breathing.

BRIGHTEN UP

Do you ever get overwhelmed with the demands of life, and then become sluggish or have difficulty concentrating? The Brighten Up exercise is designed to help you when you need to become more alert. Sluggishness and poor concentration are often the unwanted by-products of the anxiety related to stress. Once all that nervousness related to stress dissipates we often feel worn-out. When we feel this way, we need something that will brighten our minds so we can become alert and focused. The brighten-up exercise is designed to do just that! All you have to do to complete this exercise is to:

Vigorously rub your hands together for one minute.

When you vigorously rub your hands together you are stimulating nerve endings in the palms that signal neuro-pathways in your brain that help you feel more alert.

Tom, a marketing representative, found this was a great way to release stress at his sales team meetings. He would rub his hands vigorously under the table and no one even knew what he was doing. "After I rub my hands I feel more alert and refreshed." Tom is able to feel re-energized and more motivated to promote his business.

LIGHTEN-UP

"Hearty laughter is a good way to jog internally without having to go outdoors. It enhances respiration. It is an igniter of great expectations," says Norman Cousins.

Norman Cousins, editor and noted author of *Anatomy of an Illness*, revealed to the world the healing power of laughter, which allows us to feel refreshed and relaxed. It boosts our immune system, and our hope. Laughter can quickly revive us from the burdensome effects of stress.

Bob an executive director of a social service agency reported that after one week this exercise changed his approach to managing his employees and himself. "I've always been too serious on the job. I push my employees and myself too hard. Laughing with them has changed my rough exterior. When I take time out to connect with my colleagues for the purpose of laughter the day goes by more smoothly, and the work still gets done!" Bob adapted the laughter exercise to his own personal style, and sought out opportunities every day to laugh with his employees. You may want to take Bob's lead and do the same or you may want to simply laugh out loud by yourself for one minute. Either way when you take time out to - *laugh out loud for one minute* - you will be doing the Lighten Up exercise.

LOOSEN-UP

Have you ever come home after a long day at work with a tense neck, shoulders, or back? If you have this tension is probably a physical response to stress. Our bodies brace themselves automatically when we feel threatened - the fight or flight response. Bracing our bodies is a physical reaction to stress. We automatically do this repeatedly throughout a day. This response is unconscious, but we become aware of soreness resulting from these automatic physiological reaction to stress. This pain is usually stored in our neck, shoulders, and back. The loosen-up exercise is designed to release this stored up tension. To loosen-up I have created a one minute silly dance exercise. Yes that's right silly dance!

Many of us have that undeveloped dance move that shows up on the dance floor when we least expect it. It's the move the makes us feel cool, but everyone else thinks it makes us look like a geek. If we were honest with ourselves the move makes us feel silly and innocent. Have you ever watched a two-year old dance? Two-year olds have the silly dancing down pat. They haven't developed the ability to coordinate the movement of their legs, arms and trunks at the same time, so they move their legs, then arms, and then sway. To do this exercise:

Mimic the movements of a two-year old, or do your own natural silly dance moves for one minute.

Colleen is a businesswoman who recently got a promotion she didn't expect. Her boss is dictatorial and she hasn't quite gotten the handle of her new position despite doing it for several months. She attributes these difficulties to the fact that when she took the promotion, "They decided to change the whole department. No one in the company knew what my new role would be. No one could train me because no one had ever done my job. I've had to learn the whole job by myself. It's been very stressful and frustrating." Colleen decided to do the silly dance for her Take a Break and Re-energize exercise. "It really helps me to feel calm and relaxed" she reflects. "I close my office door and do my thing," she adds.

Bob decided after laughing produced such good results he'd try the silly dance. "I found it helped me at the end of the day to transition from work to home life. Over the weekend I took time out to put my groove on at home. For the first time in my life I danced for me and it was great! Now when I do something that makes me happy I get up and do a little dance. Everyone thinks it's silly but I feel great!"

PICKING THE RIGHT RE-ENERGIZING EXERCISE

Which one of the four Take a Break and Re-energizing exercises will work best for you? The decision is entirely based on your personal preferences. What matters most is picking one to work with and trying it out for a week or two. It is perfectly all right to experiment with each exercise to discover which one fits your style. I recommend, however, that if you are going to experiment with any of these exercises that you stick with it for one week before trying another one. Take a moment to reflect on which exercise you think would be the most comfortable for you to do, or randomly pick one before moving onto the next chapter.

Chapter V

CREATE SOMETHING NEW

SIMPLE CREATIVE ACTIVITIES LIKE doodling, rhyming, or singing allow us to alter our perceptions in order to see the hidden beauty in ordinary life. When we create something new we connect to the spontaneity of life. We see first hand that life is constantly changing. We learn to connect to our intuition. Intuition is the ability to know something or discover something without thinking about it. The creativity exercises are designed to get you to think in another direction, in order to recognize the beauty that already exists within you.

Creating Something New helps to build the virtue of belief in the supernatural. Believing in the supernatural occurs when you feel that you are connecting to something beyond your normal everyday experience. The act of creating requires you to trust in your abilities, to engage in an artistic activity, and to witness the results. Creating for the sake of itself will

allow you to reach beyond your normal routine and connect
to the extraordinary.

Creating Something New is akin to personal bliss, but the
process of engaging in a creative act may be intimidating.
Do you remember being very young and enjoying coloring,
singing, or playing with great glee? Have you seen your own
or other people's children be so imaginative that you are awed
by their innate creativity?

Connecting to your own innate creativity may feel foreign.
This awkward feeling is like watching guys who have trouble
dancing. This clumsiness is often the result of years of believing
that you aren't good enough to express yourself artistically. "I
can only draw stick figures." "I sing off tune," you may lament.
These limiting expressions often reflect external messages we
were told as youngsters to redirect our energy and attention to
those activities that we were most talented at, or had the most
potential for. Our parents and teachers through no fault of
their own encouraged us to be athletic, academic, or social.
Creative expression is often saved for the prodigies. Prodigies
display exceptional artistic talent. As a result the majority
of us were encouraged to engage in creativity as a form of
play that we would eventually outgrow. Many grown-ups
see their capacity for artistic expression as silly, childlike,
underdeveloped, or inept. These misunderstandings about
our own abilities to be creative limit our ability to be happy.
These distorted perceptions often reinforce those very cycles
that keep us stuck in our problems, and prevent us from
finding solutions that liberate us and allow us to feel free.

Creativity is a vital element in those personalities that

are able to reproduce auto-hypnosis in their lives. These people recognize the importance of thinking outside the box in order to accomplish the inconceivable. They routinely challenge themselves to engage in creative activities. Their ability to be creative is an essential ingredient to experiencing happiness.

When we tell ourselves we are not creative we are boxing ourselves into to a reality with limited options. To be happy, we need to know that there is an unlimited potential of options available to us in our everyday lives. Creative activities allow us to recognize we have the capacity to profit from our ordinary experience. The Create Something New exercise is designed to help you learn how to harness the power of artistic expression.

When we recognize our ability to reach beyond our normal lives and to give birth to something new we touch upon the supernatural. Each creative exercise will allow you to develop a sense of curiosity about your own ability to be more artistic. These exercises promote ingenuity by helping you learn how to make new things within a moment. Engaging in creativity permits you to appreciate the beauty that is around you. A flower, a rhythm, even two words that rhyme all present opportunities to perceive normal experience as graceful. These exercises are designed to be fun and promote a humorous response to life. The ability to appreciate your own potential to create may allow you to feel closer to the force behind all creation; this appreciation may in turn promote your own spirituality.

If you want to eliminate cognitive distortions that tell

you that you are stuck in the same routines, learning to be a creative thinker will help. The Take a Break to be Creative exercise combats cognitive distortions and promotes positive self-care traits. The four creative exercises are designed to spark your curiosity about your own artistic potential. Being creative will inspire a playful attitude and better appreciation of your own innate talents.

Most importantly, as you develop a habit of daily creativity you will be more prone to ingenious thinking, and less likely to be stuck in the cyclical patterns of cognitive distortions. The four Take a Break to be Creative exercises are; Sing, Sing a Tune, Doodle, Silly Rhymes, and Invent Something New.

SING, SING A TUNE

Sing, sing a tune, you probably remember a childhood song or popular hit that makes you feel happy whenever you hear it. This assignment is inspired by the positive response music creates to your mood. Music is a positive mood adjuster. Nearly everyone enjoys listening to some type of music. A daily practice of singing, humming, or whistling will promote happiness, and you may find it so easy and enjoyable to do that it will brighten your day.

At my family's Christmas celebration in 2005, my mother asked if the five of her nine children who were present, plus spouses and grandchildren, and a hodge-podge of other relatives would sing Christmas Carols. I possess a horrific singing voice so singing out loud for me is awkward. But being able to oblige my mother's request brought great joy to her and all who were present. I can honestly say that that Christmas was one of the best I have ever had with my family, because we sang together.

When we sing, hum, or whistle a unique composition and/or adaptation of a favorite tune, we breathe deeply and this alone increases the oxygen level in our blood stream. We know from the Slow Down exercise that deep breathing promotes clear thinking. You don't have to be a classically trained singer to enjoy creating your own tunes—I'm not. But if you choose this exercise you may find the incredible joy derived from one minute of whistling, humming, or singing.

If you choose Sing, sing, a tune as your Create Something New exercise I want to challenge you to avoid using actual words. Instead, use silly words like "la, la, la or fa, tee, la." Nonsense is essential here. This exercise will help you clear your mind of thoughts and worries so that you are able to renew yourself and think in a different direction. To perform this exercise:

Simply sing, hum or whistle your personal composition or adaptation of your favorite tune for one minute.

DOODLE

Tony Buzan has made a career out of teaching people how to doodle. In his book, *The Mind Map Book*, he explains his technique for enhancing memory and improving note-taking skills. Mind mapping is deliberate and focused doodling. Buzan reveals the neuro-science behind the memory of images and color, and the biological obstacles we face when processing black letters on white paper. Our brains remember images more readily than written ideas or concepts, according to Buzan. When we doodle we reinforce our natural perceptual tendencies to retain vital information.

Doodling is a challenging task for those who are unfamiliar with its rewards. Many of us have been told repeatedly or have witnessed the telling of others that doodling is distracting our ability to pay attention. According to Buzan this advice is contrary to how our brains really process information. Doodling engages the brain and allows us retain more information.

Doodling requires us to overcome the negative messages we have gotten in the past about its destructive nature, and allows us to explore the world of stick figures and geometric shapes. If doodling is the creative exercise you select:

Grab a pen and paper and doodle away, but remember only doodle for one minute.

SILLY RHYMES

When I met Larry, the retired steelworker, he was pretty down and out. He was recovering from a recent surgery. His focus was outward on all the world's troubles. He described his life as a failure. He felt alone, and depressed. But then Larry started to talk about the rhymes he had composed ever since he was in high school primarily as an expression of love for his family, and his faith in God. As Larry recited his poetry he transformed right before my eyes. This very depressed man became animated and joyful. When he recited his poetry he presented a delightful innocence that exposed a youthful interior, while also revealing a profound wisdom that many would live lifetimes to achieve. Here's one of Larry's lyrics: "When will I really be glad? When I become a man like my dad!" Larry stated, "You're going to think I'm crazy" before reciting his first rhyme to me. Thankfully this cognitive distortion that he was crazy stopped by his third week into my happiness program. By then he had started to see his rhyming abilities as a special gift.

Toni, the beautician and business owner, found this exercise to be delightful. "When I find myself bored with a business meeting I'll make up rhymes about the people in the room. I was stuck in traffic and I made up this jingle "I'm in my car, it used to take me to the bar, now I go far." As Toni went through her happiness program something magical happened to her rhyming exercise. She discovered her own internal rhythm. She described it as a drum beat. Here is her explanation of what happened. "I was doing my rhyming when I noticed I was also breathing deeply, so I switched to deep breathing and this drum beat started going off in my head. So I went with it, I started deep breathing and composing this rhythm. I felt so alive when I did this. I felt so much in the here and now, and it was in me all this time I just didn't realize it until now."

Both Larry and Toni's experience with rhyming allowed them to be creative in their own intuitive way. Larry had rhymed since high school, but was told by his friends and family that his rhymes were silly so he stopped sharing them with others, and internalized them as his "crazy" hobby. Toni found it to be a tool to ease boredom, and then adapted the exercise to fit her natural style. When I taught them the power of this simple one minute exercise their results were liberating.

As nearly all of my exercises are, this one is simply done. I suggested to Toni to start by looking around her environment, and pick an object she saw, like a "pen." Then I suggested she start by thinking about words that rhyme with pen, hen, ten, men, etc. As she progressed with the exercise she naturally started to compose little poems or sayings. To do the rhyming exercise simply:

Pick an object/word and find other words that rhyme with it and do this for a minute. As you get used to rhyming words it is natural for some people to compose little poems or limericks, but this is not necessary. If you just rhyme words for one minute each day that will suffice.

INVENT SOMETHING NEW

If there could be a universal characteristic to describe the self-propelling personality it would be the ability to think outside of the box. Inventive thinking reinforces happiness. Inventors are the quintessential original thinkers. Invention is an American heritage. From original thinkers like Jefferson and his contemporaries to Thomas Edison, Henry Ford, and so on, the American penchant for invention has been and remains the envy of the rest of the world.

When we invent we take a thought of how we could do something easier, or better, or that will help others and build on it. Invention is often the adaptation of someone else's idea. Henry Ford didn't invent the car; he invented a better way to make a car. Bill Gates didn't invent the computer; he invented a better operating system so that more people could easily use computers. To practice this exercise I am asking you to think about inventing something new or improving something that already exists, all in one minute. You may write out your ideas if it helps. You may choose to make this exercise cumulative, by developing your idea over a couple of days or weeks. When you practice the Invent Something New exercise:

> *Develop a new idea about a gadget or process that will help you or others do something easier or more efficiently. You may elect to build on your idea by adding new dimensions to it day by day, or start from scratch each day you invent.*

It is not necessary to invent something for patent. This exercise is intended to stimulate creative thinking. However, if you do invent something that gets patented - great!

Denise had a lot of difficulty with this exercise. Her sexually abusive father had instilled in her a belief that she was not mechanically inclined. With some counseling she decided to invent "a block" to prevent this negative message she heard every time she tried to practice this exercise. Her "block" was literally to clear her mind. She stated, "My dad always said 'You're not mechanical, you couldn't even find your way out of a box.' Her father's negative criticism about her not being mechanical, by the way, is an example of how some cognitive distortions get started. Denise stated that she is terrible at driving directions as well, but "I always find my way home," she said with a laugh. She has an ingenious way of looking at her sense of direction. Her ability to find her way home and her humor about how she goes about finding her way is purposeful and effective.

Denise's cognitive distortion that she couldn't find her way out of a box works as a barrier preventing her from recognizing her own unique sense of direction. A week later, Denise decided her second invention would be to tell herself when she was getting anxious driving in the car, to calm down and believe that she was going to find her way. "Now, I'm finding parking spaces that weren't there a minute ago, and actually feeling more calm and in control when I'm driving somewhere." Denise learned to invent concepts and behaviors that allowed her to feel calm and confident in regards to an activity that always produced stress due to her own cognitive distortion about her abilities. Denise's example demonstrates how simple and profound this exercise can be in regards to changing cognitive distortions and producing positive new self perceptions. She learned to feel more confident and secure with herself and her potential.

When we are confident about our ability to think outside the box and be ingenious we will experience greater freedom. All we have to do is to try to invent and believe that we will benefit from our efforts.

CHOOSING YOUR CREATIVE EXERCISE

To choose the Create Something New exercises that will work for you may want to use the system you devised with the Take a Break and Re-energize exercise group or create a new way of deciding which one of Sing, Sing a Tune, Doodle, Silly Rhymes, or Invent Something New you want to incorporate into your day to day life. You may decide the best way to pick one is to try each out and see which one fits best for you. The important thing is to pick an exercise and then try it out for a week or two, before trying another one. Take a second to reflect on how you are going to select an exercise from this group, and if possible choose one now before going to the next chapter.

Chapter VI

LEARN SOMETHING NEW

IT WAS 1995 AND I was working for a hospice in Tucson, Arizona. During one particular visit with a terminally ill woman her daughter told me "no day is wasted if you learn something new." I was surprised by the common sense wisdom in this statement and asked the daughter where she learned such a profound thing. She pointed to her mother. Each person has moments in their lives where someone else gives them a precious ounce of wisdom. One of the greatest attributes of life is the ability to help others persevere. Every teacher needs a student, and developing a willingness to learn new things each day will create incredible opportunities to profit from others.

Not only will learning something new from others each day allow us to be wiser by promoting the virtue of loving others. Being able to learn from others, and appreciate the help we receive each day, is a vitally important aspect of how we experience joy. The learning exercises I have designed for you will help you build this virtue through the use of the four learn something new exercises.

When you take time out of your day to help someone in need even if it's holding a door open, or giving someone your seat on the bus, you are practicing kindness. When we take time out of our busy days to reflect on the gifts others have given us in life, these actions are a sign of our love others, and our love for learning. Forgiveness is a liberating act of letting go of past resentments or betrayals, and saying to ourselves these feelings of hatred and ill will help no one and least of all ourselves. When we are able to learn from others, we are better able to be fair with our-selves and as a result we feel happier.

These exercises include opportunities to be more generous, to appreciate others' kindness, to recognize the lessons from negative interactions, and to learn from forgiveness. When you routinely engage in these learning exercises you will gain the wisdom to analyze your interactions with others, decide how you want to be perceived, and manage how you want to relate to others. The lessons learned will directly impact your actions, and will be recognized by others. Learning from others will allow you to be a wiser, more loving, and self-fulfilled person.

The Learn Something New exercises is focused on promoting those virtues of wisdom and knowledge, and loving others. These exercises work to contradict cognitive distortions we hold about the world as cruel and unjust, where only the morally corrupt succeed. When you become used to learning something new from *others*, you will see that the

great majority of us care for each other. Those unfortunates
that create hardships out of spite, greed, or their own misery
can be great teachers—of how not to behave. There are four
distinct exercises in this group, so be prepared to identify your
preferences at the end of this section.

APPRECIATE A TEACHER

We all have someone that has taught us powerful lessons
about life, like the daughter of that hospice patient I visited
in Tucson. Her lesson was that no day was wasted if you "learn
something new." Her mother was the person who had taught
her this powerful lesson. Appreciating the lessons people have
taught us is a vital happiness tool. When we're blue, we often
focus our attention on what others are doing to make our
lives miserable. One way to overcome the false perception
that other people are causing our misery is to take time out to
appreciate those who have been there for us when the chips
were down.

Throughout my life I have been blessed with a wide variety
of teachers. Here is a sample of some of my greatest teachers.
My father taught me how to be disciplined and the importance
of hard work. He taught me how to focus my attention and to
be an analytical thinker. My mother taught me gentler things
like the importance of daily prayer, how to enjoy the outdoors,
how to play games, and the importance of cleanliness.

Another powerful role model was my grade school cross-
country coach. He taught me the importance of endurance,
and stick-to-it-ness. There was the Catholic priest in college

who encouraged me to get honest with myself about my drinking problem. As a result I was able to benefit from drug and alcohol treatment where the counselors taught me to recognize my addiction and taught me tools I could use to stay sober. There have been countless numbers of other recovering addicts who have encouraged and helped me along my road of recovery. College professors have served as mentors for my chosen career, and sparked my passion for psychology and personal empowerment. My wife has been an incredible teacher in how to appreciate the beauty in life and perceiving life as an adventure. My son has taught me to see the world as a new and exciting place as well as the value of spontaneous play. I would need to include employers and supervisors who have taught me valuable work skills, and friends and siblings who have taught me the value of companionship, and encouragement. If I wanted to, I could probably list hundreds of people who have taught me valuable lessons that have enhanced my quality of life and my confidence to persevere through tough times.

You also have many teachers who have helped you along your road in life. Developing the ability to reflect on the lessons you have received from others will allow you to see that many people in your world have invested time and energy in your potential for success. Appreciating others' contributions to your well-being can enhance your sense of satisfaction with your own life.

The opportunities to learn from others are endless. Have you ever noticed people at the grocery store or in traffic that do kind deeds to absolute strangers? We are so busy getting frustrated with the rude and obnoxious people in life that we often ignore or minimize random acts of kindness that occur around us all the time. We expect people to be obnoxious and rude, and therefore they are. We are used to being angry and disappointed with people and so it is easier to feel anger and disappointment with them. These expectations and feelings, although unpleasant, give us a false sense of security and control, because they have a predictability factor. Choosing to appreciate everyday teachers will allow you to undermine this common societal belief, that we can't trust each other and that people are only looking out for themselves.

In order to do this exercise you will need to:

List seven of your most powerful teachers that have positively influenced your life. In the space below list each of these teachers, and the lessons they taught you.

Seven of my teachers in life have been: *The Lessons they taught me:*

1. _____   _____
2. _____   _____
3. _____   _____
4. _____   _____
5. _____   _____
6. _____   _____
7. _____   _____

For the next seven days select one of these teachers and the corresponding lesson you learned and take one minute to reflect on the person and lesson and what this has meant to your betterment. At the end of your first week list seven more great teachers that you admire or routinely help you. As time progresses you may choose to trust that you will find new teachers each day who will provide lessons on the importance of loving others, and/or reinforce your own passion for learning.

GENEROSITY & COMPASSION

Recognize this saying: "Practice random acts of kindness"? Well, purposely making an attempt each day to show compassion or help someone out will go a long way in promoting your happiness. Jesse, the guy who thinks hot women and fast cars is where happiness is, tried being kind to strangers for one week. He reported, "It was so nice to see that person's face light up and to see someone smile when I told her how nice she looked, or how much I appreciated her service."

Denise stated, "I feel so warm inside when I compliment someone for no other reason but to be nice to them." Helping out a stranger by letting them go first in line at the grocery store or giving someone in need a dollar can go a long way in promoting the development of the virtue of loving others.

Often people very close to us suffer from the effects of stress or depression. Their distress may be caused by their own cognitive distortion, but our little acts of kindness can promote happiness in their lives as well, by letting them know someone really does care. Here are some examples of how random acts of kindness can lift your spirits. Take time out to compliment your coworkers, neighbors, and friends. Tell others how much you appreciate them for the things they do for you. Take time out to thank clerks in stores, a receptionist, or other service people for their hard work and explain how their efforts enrich your life. Each of these examples demonstrates ways that you can practice generosity and compassion. The opportunities to be generous and compassionate are endless. This is my guide for how to practice the Generosity and Compassion exercise:

Write out a list of people to whom or places where you can practice being kind or generous to in the next week. In the space below list seven opportunities where you can be kind or giving to others.

My personal list of generous and compassionate opportunities:

1. _____
2. _____
3. _____
4. _____
5. _____
6. _____
7. _____

Now practice one of these seven opportunities from your list above each day for the next week.

LEARN FROM THE NEGATIVE

I once had a job where my immediate supervisor was a tyrant. He was so domineering and insensitive that very few of his employees had any respect for him. He would often criticize the clients we served, and/or humiliate his employees. I was in a place in my life where I needed a job and benefits more then professional supervision.

I stayed at that job four long years, and during that time I learned a lot about myself and about how to deal with a very difficult person—my boss. Maybe you have also had difficult, mean, and/or tyrannical people with whom you have had to deal? If you have, these types of people may provide you with a well of riches that you never expected to find Mean people can be diamonds in the rough. Picture a difficult person in your own life and ask yourself "what lesson am I supposed to learn from this person?" Reflect on your intuitive answer to this question. It may be patience, or compassion, or that you need to find the courage to move in another direction in your relationships or career. The lesson I learned from my supervisor was that I needed to praise myself for a job well done, and not expect my superiors to always or even ever appreciate my work.

Another approach towards learning from those who annoy you is to challenge yourself to appreciate a positive attribute this person possesses that you don't have. Often the reason we find these types of people so annoying is that in some way they reflect strengths or talents we wish we had. Ask yourself, "What strengths does this person have that I wish I could have?"

Then, reflect on your intuitive answer. You may find that your intuitive response will allow you to soften your attitude to this person.

Another reason we find people annoying or difficult to work with is that they have a negative behavior that we also have. We can learn from negative people by being determined to correct the behaviors in ourselves that are mirrored in our Negative Person. For instance, I am irritated by people who are always grabbing the spotlight because I want the spotlight—all the time. When I meet someone who mirrors my negative attributes, it reminds me to work on my own personality. We sometimes project on others our own faults, as well.

Learning from negative interactions can create many opportunities for finding serenity. Negative people are often perceived as threats, and interactions or even thoughts of interacting with these people can produce stress. As discussed earlier, stress reactions can create more problems. Learning to face negative people with an open or reflective mind will allow us to discover how to profit from some one else's negativity.

In the book *Man's Search for Meaning*, Victor Frankl, a concentration camp survivor and physician, described how he realized that the only thing the Nazis couldn't control was his attitude, and he wasn't going to let them undermine his spirit or his will to survive. Frankl's message is that when faced with adversity and negativity we still have a choice about how we respond. In order to Learn From the Negative:

You will need to write out seven situations or people that you perceive as negative, in the space provided and follow the instructions that appear below.

The 7 situations/people I routinely encounter as negative:

1. _____
2. _____
3. _____
4. _____
5. _____
6. _____
7. _____

Now that you have a list, plan to practice facing each one of these situations in the next seven days, but with the attitude of learning and self-discovery. Tell yourself, "I am going to face so & so or this situation, but when I am in his presence, I'll ask myself what do I need to learn from this person?" Then observe yourself and see how you respond. You need not confront that person, just reflect on your intuitive answer about what you need to learn. It may take a couple tries before the anxiety and stress related to the negative situation dissipates. Keep at it and in time you will become aware of powerful lessons your can discover from negative interactions.

FORGIVENESS

Denise has had a lot of abuse in her life. The events of Denise's childhood and early adulthood have left significant emotional scars. However, she has learned the powerful lesson of forgiveness by not allowing the negative events of her past undermine her own natural resilience and personal strengths. Denise learned that when she focused her attention on all the injustice life had dealt her, she became paralyzed by anger and depression. She has never understood why her parents abused her. She does not condone in any way their horrific actions. What she has done is realize that being angry with them for their neglect and abuse only hurts herself. She has learned to use the healing power of forgiveness to release her from the bonds of her abusive past.

Forgiveness is a powerful tool you can learn to transform how you relate to your negative past. Forgiving others does not give permission for the injustice you suffered to continue, but rather allows you to assert your right to healing, while acknowledging the humanity of another. Humanity in all its goodness is still imperfect and unjust at times. It is intolerance, not forgiveness that reinforces these imperfections. Forgiveness strengthens goodness and justness. When we forgive we release ourselves from the shackles of resentment. So if the injustice someone has done to you is so great that your anger towards them holds you in a metaphorical prison, then you might find reflections on forgiveness as your liberator.

Allowing yourself to release the rage you feel towards past abusers, and telling yourself you will not allow their energy to continue to effect your well-being, can be very freeing. Depending on how traumatic your past harms have been, it may take several tries with each offender to feel confident you have succeeded in forgiveness. This exercise is intended to be reflective. I do not recommend that you face a perpetrator head on, and tell them "I forgive you." Here is my recommended guideline for this exercise:

Take one-minute to reflect on a past injury. If it helps, picture in your mind the offender, and say to yourself and this image, "I forgive you." When you are able to do this with a sense of ease and a calm mind you will be practicing this exercise. Learning to forgive is a powerful tool for promoting self-confidence and happiness. If you choose this exercise please list seven people that you feel have harmed you.

Seven people who have harmed me in that past who I would like to forgive:

1. _____
2. _____
3. _____
4. _____
5. _____
6. _____
7. _____

Once you have completed this list pick one offender to practice forgiving him/her for the next seven days. Don't move to the next person on your list until you feel you have comfortably acknowledged forgiveness for each person on your list. Depending on the nature of past harms it may take days, weeks, or even months to create a place in your heart for forgiveness. Don't move to the next name until you have a sense of peace and forgiveness when you reflect on that particular person.

CHOOSING A LEARN
SOMETHING NEW EXERCISE

You are now ready to decide which of the four "Learn Something New" exercises will work best with your personality. These four exercises are a little more involved then the prior three exercise groups. Experimentation is okay with this group as well, and may actually be the best way to reap the greatest benefit from my program. The more exercises you do and become comfortable doing the more positive traits you will be developing. However, because the Learn Something New Exercises are more involved then the other exercises, I recommend you try each of these exercises for at least one week at a time before switching to another exercise in this group. These four exercises can create so much joy and satisfaction in your life because of their power to promote your happiness and improve your connection to others. You need to dedicate sufficient time and effort to reap the greatest reward from each exercise. Experimentation is not for everyone, and maybe you know or have a good idea which exercise will be the most comfortable for you. Take a few moments to reflect on your choice before going to the next chapter.

Chapter VII

BE GRATEFUL AT BEDTIME

ONE OF THE BEST ways to stop hedonism is by practicing gratitude. With this life style, our happiness is dependent on obtaining possessions, status, and / or excitement. The pleasure we feel when we are focused only on pleasure depends on experiences like buying new cars, receiving promotions, or having wild sex. Once we get used to our possessions, responsibilities, or the excitement, their effects wear off, and we find ourselves wanting more. Most of us stuck in a hedonistic cycle end up feeling as if we will never have enough.

Jesse never seemed to find true happiness. He was doing his own wake-up surprised exercise for years before he and I met, reading a daily online reflection on optimism each morning when he was getting ready for his day. He enjoyed being generous and kind to others. He did not consider either activity as having the power to promote lasting happiness in his life.

The last time I saw him he was extremely excited, almost manic. He described a wild night of sex with a new partner which had brought him to the current state: "This is real happiness, I can't wait till I see her again." Jesse is only happy when he is in a cycle of hedonism. He'll tire of this new partner, because new partners eventually become the same partner. He'll continually need new and different experiences to feel the elation he desires.

Jesse has tried it all, fast cars, exciting hobbies, explicit sexual affairs—none have granted him lasting satisfaction in his life. "I can't concentrate on the things I'm grateful for each day, this program is not for me," he said. Jesse seemed to want to see me more out of curiosity about the book I was writing than to discover what would really make him happy. He never got it that he had all he needed to be happy just by being himself.

A daily gratitude practice tells us, "Yes we do have enough!" Gratitude allows us to recognize those things we have that are precious, but that we take for granted. Our homes, jobs, families, our physical abilities, and ultimately our lives are all things we can appreciate. Gratitude reveals to us that at any point in life we so much for which we can give thanks.

Reflecting each day on the blessings we have received in life is another powerful happiness tool. Each of us is unique with respect to our own abilities. When we reflect on these blessings, we find tangible proof of what makes us happy. Gratitude allows us to recognize our ability to maintain this on a day-to-day basis.

Addicts are people who get imprisoned by the pleasure

they seek, whether it is from alcohol, sex, drugs, gambling, shopping, or food. Addiction robs a person of the ability to live a life of moderation because the substance or activity becomes the primary focus in his/her life. All an addict ever thinks about is getting, having, and keeping his/her next fix. For the addict, life is a series of events supporting the pursuit of the next high. Work, relationships, recreation all rotate around this one obsession and the addict is robbed of the ability to live life on life's terms. When things don't go the addict's way in life he blames the world for betraying him and thinks about getting high. When things do go his way, he wants to make it better by getting high.

When I was hooked in my own addiction my life was this way, I woke up with my bong at my bedside, and had to take a toke before I could get out of bed. On most days I started drinking by 10 or 11 A.M. I was well on my way to oblivion by noon, and if I didn't pass out at night my bong with her sweet soft curves was always waiting for me in bed. Everything I did revolved around getting high.

In my early recovery I was introduced to many recovery tools that helped me stay sober, but one of the most powerful of these tools was gratitude. Gratitude helped me see that I had everything I needed to get by right then/now. It reinforced for me that life in and of itself is the reward. I learned through gratitude to keep my focus on what I had rather then on what I didn't. This allowed me to honor and appreciate the simple pleasures in life, a good laugh with friends, dinner with my parents, going to the movies, or a walk in the park, were all opportunities to feel grateful. As I achieved the milestones in my personal recovery one year sober, five years, sober, ten years sober, and now over twenty years sober, gratitude has not lost its power in helping me stay on the road of recovery, nor has it lost its ability to reinforce my happiness.

Gratitude is not simply a tool to help addicts stay committed to recovery it is one of the most powerful happiness tools. In fact a study conducted at the University of Pennsylvania demonstrated that doing a five minute gratitude exercise each night before sleeping dramatically increases a person's ability to feel satisfied with their life. Learning to feel grateful for what you have right now will greatly impact your ability to find happiness in everyday life.

I believe that gratitude is so powerful a quality that spending just one minute each night being thankful will transform your life into one of joy and contentment. You may find that after practicing gratitude consistently for a short time you will look towards your daily activities with a new level of appreciation. Often I appreciate a warm shower, a beautiful sunrise, a hug, or a good joke. In fact, each of the four happiness exercises, are opportunities to find gratitude in your life. By instituting the one minute gratitude exercise each night before sleeping you will be sealing your happiness goal, and making it a reality and not another unfulfilled dream.

Practicing gratitude helps us to get away from the cycle of hedonism by showing us each day that we need to be content. As long as we are alive we have the ability to be and stay happy. We are programmed to experience pleasure; our survival depends on it. Practicing gratitude is one way to achieving personal satisfaction. Here is an explanation of how to do this exercise:

> *Be Grateful at Bedtime means that each night before you prepare for bed or fall asleep, you review your day and identify the things you're most grateful for.*

I reflect on 10 things each day I'm grateful for, in a list fashion. I use my fingers to count and this practice usually takes me one minute to complete. Bob, the social service agency executive director, decided to reflect on one thing for which he was grateful each day. It was his personal high point that he cherished with a minute reflection at bedtime. In his professional life of shrinking public dollars and increasing client needs he felt the pressures of professional survival every day. He felt that each small success needed a special reflection of gratitude. You may choose to reflect on one thing like Bob or 10 things like I do, but remember to practice this exercise for one minute each night before you sleep.

Chapter VIII

THE SIMPLICITY
OF HAPPINESS

USING THE HAPPINESS EXERCISES

I ADVISE THAT YOU PRACTICE each of the five happiness exercises, by following this format: "Wake-up Surprised" within one hour of waking, "Take a Break to Re-energize" between 10:00-11:00 A.M., "Take a Break to be Creative" between two and three in the afternoon, "Learning Something New" between your commute home and 7:00 P.M., "Be Grateful at Bedtime" as you are preparing for bed, or getting into bed to sleep. This regimen will help promote happy brain chemistry throughout your day, while also contradicting the negative effects of cognitive distortions and stress. Try this regimen out for at least one month or until the exercise routine seems natural in relation to your day to day activities.

By following the five minute a day happiness exercises with this simple suggestion you should begin to notice significant changes in your overall personal satisfaction in little or no time. You will be well on your way to experiencing a happier more fulfilling life. These five one-minute happiness exercises will transform your life just as it has for so many others.

Depending on how you choose to work your five minute a day happiness program, you may find that you want to continue the regimen longer then one month. If you simply pick one exercise for each group and decide to work each of these for 28 days then there are four different programs you can choose from. These different programs are the variations of the middle three exercises.

At the end of the first month of working the same five exercises, you could select another three middle exercises to work the following month. This process is much more deliberate then experimenting with each exercise to see which best fits your personality style. However, it is an option to consider when getting started with this program.

It isn't necessary to extend the program to different designs. Toni stated that after one month she found two exercises the most helpful. These were the Take a Break to Re-energize, Slow Down exercise, and the Take a Break to be Creative exercise, Rhyming. She contributed her stress reactions as her major cause for unhappiness. Toni found that when she combined these exercises whenever she found herself tense that she was able to relax and redirect her attention on what was really important—her happiness.

It is very likely that as you progress through the first month, you may adapt some of the exercises to your own style, like Bob and Toni. That is perfectly okay. In fact I hope you will discover from these exercises your unique way of managing your life in the pursuit of happiness. The magic of this program isn't necessarily the exercises, it's what happens in between the exercises. As you perform these tasks every day, you will discover hidden talents, and strengths that help you find personal bliss.

THE SIMPLICITY OF HAPPINESS

When Thomas Jefferson wrote his famous words in the Declaration of Independence, "Life, liberty and the pursuit of Happiness," he transformed the world. Pursuing happiness has mystified and inspired Americans ever since. For some the pursuit of happiness leads to misery and disillusionment. For others who achieve happiness, many unknowingly subscribe to Jefferson's recommendations of industry, virtue, and love for others. The five one-minute happiness exercises are designed to give you easy access to developing a daily discipline that promotes these qualities. As you discover how to live life following this simple guide you will naturally develop aspects of the six universal virtues, and a daily discipline that will enhance your ability to feel happier and more satisfied with life.

IS HAPPINESS SIMPLE?

I have given you the fundamentals of several very complex ideas, in order to expedite your understanding of what it takes to be happy. Happiness, its pursuit, the obstacles that prevent us from achieving it, and the qualities that promote it can all be complicated themes. We have reviewed what prevents happiness—polar extremes of hedonism and depression. These opposite positions seem to be hinged on personal beliefs that distort reality. I have discussed rudimentary aspects of neuro-biology, solution directed therapy, and the concept of auto-hypnosis, to illustrate the ideas of resiliency and our natural tendency to experience pleasure to survive. To explain in detail all of these topics and others that have been addressed within this text would literally take volumes. My goal was to provide a basic explanation of these ideas in such a way that they could be easily understood. Hopefully, you gained a better understanding of those behaviors, thoughts, and actions that interfere with the successful pursuit of happiness, as well as those elements that promote happiness.

The simplicity of happiness goes beyond a fundamental explanation of its pros and cons. The pursuit of happiness and its obtainment is simple because it involves common sense decisions about living life. These decisions are based on where we focus our attention. If we decide that money and power are to be our focus the chance that we will find true lasting happiness becomes threatened. We may have a greater chance to afford comforts and pleasures with wealth, but wealth, power, and prestige is no guarantee for happiness. Rather if we place our focus on ourselves, and the values by which we live our lives, we will find a greater sense of contentment in life. Ultimately you will feel the wealth and power of your life right now, so that you can start living the life you have always desired.

How we define happiness will also contribute or detract from its simplicity. Happiness is the result of a well-managed life. This can be defined and learned simply. The process of self-management can present its challenges, as does any discipline. However, for those in the grips of depression or those stuck in the cycle of hedonism, their happiness solution is a misnomer. Keeping the definition of happiness simple, like Jefferson did will help you find and keep this state of mind.

The happiest people are those who have learned to manage their own lives. The thrills they get out of life come from their ability to experience joy from activities the rest of us consider mundane. To these individuals happiness and its attainment is a simple process. They have learned to accept life on its terms, and create opportunities from its challenges. To them happiness is the natural product of a well-managed life.

Others have complicated definitions of happiness. To them it is the impossible goal that reinforces their disillusionment with life. Or it is a constantly changing goal line. Those who are disillusioned are always starting the game from the one yard line with ninety-nine to go. Those chasing the impossible goal are at the ten-yard line with their goal in sight, but they never seem to get to their destination. The one yard-er's never seem to have the momentum to get beyond the first play, and often just give up hope that happiness is obtainable. The ten and goal-er's have the motivation and drive, but just when they are about to win the game, they change the game plan and they are right back at tenth and goal. These folks are always saying, "one more accomplishment, and then I'll be happy." Happiness is obscure for these folks who are at the polar opposites of depression and hedonism, but they have a commonality in that they have distorted perceptions of the "pursuit of happiness." Their distorted perception creates a complicated definition of happiness and how to pursue it.

For others happiness is simple, they simply take no responsibility for their life or actions. These individuals look towards others and/or other things for their happiness. When life does go their way, they are happy, and when it doesn't they are unhappy. It is always easier to blame others for life not turning out the way you want it. But when happiness only requires a change in perception inwards to oneself, the alternative of blame does not seem a viable excuse for not achieving personal happiness.

Yet many do not see a change of perception as a feasible option. They would prefer to stay stuck in their own cyclical problems, rather than change their direction of thinking to find a solution.

Still there are others who are struggling with serious mental illness, substance abuse issues, or may be a danger to themselves or others. This book is not recommended as a sole care option for people wrestling with these issues. If you feel you have a serious mental illness, are an addict, or are thinking of harming yourself or another my recommendation is that you request help from your physician or local mental health specialist immediately. This book may be used as a supplemental treatment tool for these conditions under the guidance or direction of a mental health care practitioner.

CAN SETTING AND ACHIEVING GOALS BE A MEANS TOWARDS ACHIEVING HAPPINESS?

Setting and achieving goals can and does promote happiness when the pleasure is derived from the activity and not solely on the outcome. Dreams are vitality. The danger is when we make happiness contingent on obtaining the dream rather than the lessons and rewards gained along the way. I have always found it easier to accomplish my goals when I break them down to their smallest elements. But before I could even dream or set goals, I had to believe my dreams were possible. Being able to be happy the majority of the time will empower you to not only dream, but also possess the belief and momentum to realize your dreams.

That's why I believe it so vital to be happy first. When we face life on its terms we are able to see new events as opportunities for growth and greater happiness. We don't necessarily look to achievement as the end product of happiness; rather we see that the journey produces joy as we progress to our final destination. When we have the tools to embrace the journey we are able to adjust our goals to the unpredictable future. We celebrate obstacles, we redefine our expectations, and we create new solutions or ideals about our dreams.

I have provided you with a program of fourteen unique

exercises that you can use within a moment's notice to redirect your attention away from the blame game, hedonism, or cognitive distortions, and back on your own innate resiliency and ability to feel happy. Use these exercises to find your bliss. Feel happy, realize your dreams, so that you can know the true meaning of the pursuit of happiness.

ACKNOWLEDGMENTS

THERE ARE MANY LOVED ones, family members, friends, colleagues, and clients who have helped me by inspiring me to write this book. I thank all of you for the lessons you have taught me. This book would not exist if it were not for my meeting and working with Eliot Jay Rosen in Tucson in the mid-1990's. Eliot's goal of writing and his metaphorical explanation of why he wrote struck home with me. He inspired in me a desire to move past my struggles and to use writing as an implement of salvation.

My partner and spouse Deb has been very instrumental in fostering and encouraging me to pursue my dreams. She has supported me in my darkest days of doubt and in my most manic days of tangential ideas and tapping keys as the pages seemingly wrote themselves. Without her support I would not have persevered with my goal. Deb, I feel blessed by your presence in my life and by your love for me, thank you.

My sister Heidi helped at the beginning of this book by

being enthusiastic at a time when I needed a cheerleader. Her support and encouragement got the ball rolling in regards to writing on happiness. My brother Eric helped with the middle part of the book by editing my first draft and providing critical analysis of my writing and content of this book. My sister Karen helped with the end of the book by editing the final draft, and encouraging with the publication process. In the eleventh hour as I prepared to submit my manuscript for its final printing my Aunt Catherine and brother in law Claire Wheeler made a convincing argument for some final editing their encouragement although unexpected was valuable and greatly appreciated. My entire family has been very helpful in encouraging my dreams, and I am blessed to have such a talented and dynamic family.

I needed a place and volunteers to conduct my study on whether or not my happiness program really helped people. That's where Sue Drey of the Pennsylvania Center for Intuitive Studies came in. Sue runs a holistic education and counseling center in Reading, Pennsylvania. Sue donated the space and solicited volunteers for my study. Her help was invaluable in getting the anecdotal stories that are woven throughout this book. Without her help this book would have never matured to its complete form.   I am deeply grateful for her spirit and support in encouraging me to pursue my dreams.

The process of writing a book is one thing, preparing it for print is entirely another. Bob Powers and the Staff at RJ Communications have been an incredible resource and guide in this phase of my writing. Their direction has helped me understand the complexities of preparing a book for market.

I feel indebted to them for their patient, generosity, and encouragement.

No book would be complete without an audience. You the reader are to be credited for wanting to find a practical resource in the instruction of achieving happiness. You are entitled to this resource. It can and will help you in finding happiness and promoting your satisfaction in life. Without your desire to find happiness, this book would have no meaning and would have never been written. Thank you for believing in your own ability to finding your bliss.

REFERENCES

Spirituality & Psychology: Care of Self, Spirit & Soul, J & K
   Seminars Lancaster, PA 6/28 &6/29, 2004 Thomas
   Moore, Ph.D.

Experiencing the Soul, Eliot Jay Rosen, Hay House, April 1998.

Light and Liberty: Reflections on the Pursuit of Happiness,
   Thomas Jefferson; Edited by Eric S. Peterson, The
   Modern Library New York, Random House Publishing
   Group, 2004.

The Pursuit of Happiness, Robert Darnton, Wilson Quarterly,
   Autumn 95 Vol. 19, Issue 5.

Finding Flow, Mihaly Csikentmihalyi, Basic Books, 1997.

Authentic Happiness, Martin Segliman, Simon & Schuster,
   Inc., 2002.

Depression, Aaron T. Beck, Harber & Row Publishers, 1967.
   Copyright University of Pennsylvania Press, 1972.

Keys to Solutions in Therapy, Steve de Shazar, W.W. Norton &
   Company, Inc., 1985.

"What the Bleep Do wΣ (k)Πow!?," William Arntz,
    Betsy Chasse, and Mark Vicente, Health
    Communications, Inc., 2005.

Bodily Changes in Pain, Hunger, Fear and Rage: An
    Account of Recent Researches into the Function of
    Emotional Excitement, W.B. Cannon, Appleton, New
    York, 1915

Anatomy of an Illness, Norman Cousins, W.W. Norton & Co,
    Inc., 1979,

*The Mind Map Book: How to Use Radiant Thinking to Maximize
    Your Brain's Untapped Potential,* Tony and Barry Buzan,
    1996 E. P. Dutton, 1994.

Man's Search for Meaning, Viktor Frankl, first published in
    1946, First translation Beacon Press, 1959, copyright
    Beacon Press, 2006.

.